A is for the aquarium that makes the Chattanooga news.

T is for Tennessee

E.J. Sullivan

Illustrated by
Neal Cross

SWEETWATER
PRESS

SWEETWATER
PRESS

T is for Tennessee
Copyright © 2006 by Sweetwater Press
Produced by Cliff Road Books

ISBN-13: 978-1-58173-527-7
ISBN-10: 1-58173-527-8

All rights reserved. With the exception of brief quotations in critical reviews or articles, no part of this work may be reproduced or transmitted in any form or by any means, electronic or mechanical, including photocopying, recording, or any information storage and retrieval system, without permission in writing from the publisher.

Printed in China

T is for Tennessee

A STATE ALPHABET BOOK

B is for Beale Street, where they sing the blues.

C is for Country –
we gave it its name.

D is for Davy Crockett, of frontier fame.

E is for Elvis, who built Graceland his way.

F is for eating fried food (almost) every day.

G is for the Grand Ole Opry, live on stage.

H is for summer heat, even in the shade.

I is for the infield at the Bristol race.

J is for Andrew
Jackson's home place.

K is for Knoxville, where we visit Aunt Daisy.

L is for the long drive on I-40 that makes Dad crazy.

M is for the mighty Mississippi River.

N is for Nashville, where the bright lights make me shiver.

O is for the Ocoee we go rafting down.

P is for the Peabody, where the ducks swim around.

Q is for the quilting ribbons Grandma won at the fair.

R is for Ruby Falls – have you ever been there?

S is for the Smokies,
where we go on vacation.

T is for the Titans, our big league sensation!

U is for UT, go Vols, go!

V is for Vanderbilt, where Uncle Joe studied law.

W is for Gramps' Walking Horse we call Mr. Brown.

Y is for Yes! We love Tennessee the bes[t]

From **Z** back to **A** it tops all the rest!